SCHOLASTIC News

Nonfiction Readers

From Eye to Potato

by Ellen Weiss

Children's Press®
A Division of Scholastic Inc.
New York Toronto London Auckland Sydney
Mexico City New Delhi Hong Kong
Danbury, Connecticut

These content vocabulary word builders are for grades 1–2.

Consultant: Pati Vitt, PhD, The Institute for Plant Conservation Biology, Chicago Botanic Garden, Glencoe, Illinois

Reading Consultant: Cecilia Minden-Cupp, PhD, Early Literacy Consultant and Author, Chapel Hill, North Carolina

Book Design: Simonsays Design!
Book Production: The Design Lab

Library of Congress Cataloging-in-Publication Data
Weiss, Ellen, 1949–
From eye to potato / by Ellen Weiss.
    p. cm.—(Scholastic news nonfiction readers)
Includes bibliographical references and index.
ISBN-13: 978-0-531-18535-3 (lib.) 978-0-531-18788-3 (pbk.)
ISBN-10: 0-531-18535-4 (lib.) 0-531-18788-8 (pbk.)
1. Potatoes—Juvenile literature. I. Title. II. Series.
SB211.P8W326 2007
635'.21—dc22   2007004487

CONTENTS

WORD HUNT

Look for these words as you read. They will be in **bold**.

eyes
(eyez)

seeds
(seedz)

seed potatoes
(seed puh-**tay**-tohz)

fruits
(froots)

roots
(roots)

sprouts
(sprouts)

tubers
(**too**-burz)

Yum! Potatoes!

How do you like to eat your potatoes? Mashed? Baked?

People eat potatoes in many parts of the world.

Potatoes grow in many places, too.

They grow in a very interesting way.

What happens when you store a potato too long?

Little white **sprouts** start growing out of the potato.

They grow from the **eyes** of the potato.

They aren't good to eat.

But they are good for growing new potatoes!

These eyes can't see,
but they can grow.

eyes

sprouts

9

New potato plants can grow from eyes.

The sprout is the beginning of a new plant.

It gets bigger and starts to grow leaves.

You don't need seeds to grow potato plants.

How does a sprout turn into a plant?

First, someone plants the sprouted potato in the ground.

Soon it will begin to grow **roots**.

The roots soak up water for the plant.

roots

Roots grow down from the plant.

Plants need food to grow.

The potato provides food to get the plant started.

Later, the plant will make new food.

It will store extra food in parts called **tubers**. Tubers can be good food for people, too.

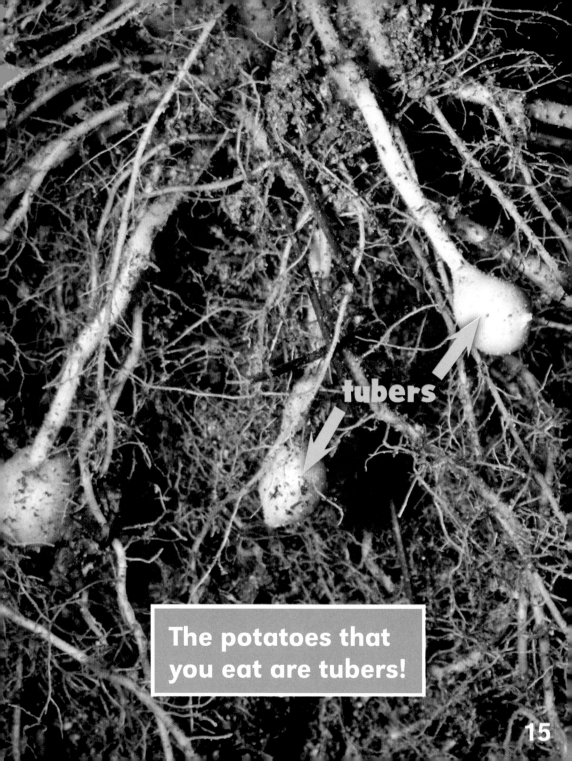

tubers

The potatoes that you eat are tubers!

Potato plants may grow flowers and **fruits**.

Potato fruits have **seeds** inside.

Farmers usually plant sprouted potatoes instead of potato seeds. They call these potatoes **seed potatoes**.

seeds

seed potatoes

16

potato
fruits

Never eat a potato fruit.
It can make you sick!

Find a potato in your kitchen.

Put it in a warm place with lots of light.

Plant it when the eyes grow sprouts.

Take good care of it.

Someday, you can eat potatoes you grow yourself.

Yum!

Dig up your potato plants to find the potatoes.

POTATO LIFE CYCLE

1 A potato begins to sprout.

2 The sprouted potato, or seed potato, is planted.

5
Dig up the potato plant when the potatoes are ready for eating!

4
Special roots called tubers store food. Potatoes are tubers.

3
The potato grows roots under the soil. The potato plant appears above the soil.

21

YOUR NEW WORDS

eyes (eyez) the parts of a potato from which sprouts grow

fruits (froots) the parts of flowering plants that contain seeds

roots (roots) parts of plants that grow underground and absorb water

seeds (seedz) parts of flowering plants from which a new plant can grow

seed potatoes (seed puh-**tay**-toze) sprouted potatoes that can be used to grow new potato plants

sprouts (sprouts) new plant growth

tubers (**too**-burz) thick, underground plant stems; many kinds of tubers can be eaten

cassava
(kuh-**sah**-vuh)

jicama
(**hee**-kuh-muh)

sweet potato
(sweet puh-**tay**-toh)

water chestnut
(**waw**-tur **chest**-nut)

INDEX

FIND OUT MORE

Book:

Coy, John, and Carolyn Fisher (illustrator). *Two Old Potatoes and Me.* New York: Alfred A. Knopf, 2003.

Website:

British Potato Council
www.potatoesforschools.org.uk/

MEET THE AUTHOR

Ellen Weiss has received many awards for her books for kids. She has a garden, where she is especially good at growing weeds.